Lean Days

Lean Days

Steve McOrmond

Wolsak and Wynn . Toronto

Typeset in Goudy Oldstyle, printed in Canada by The Coach House Printing Company, Toronto.

Cover design: Coach House
Cover art © Julian Forrest, 2001, "Dark Clouds", 45 x 55" Acrylic on canvas
Author's photograph © Janet Hoops

Some of these poems have appeared in *The Antigonish Review, echolocation, Event, The Fiddlehead, Gaspereau Review, Grain, Landmarks: An Anthology of New Atlantic Canadian Poetry of the Land, Malahat Review, Poetry Canada, Pottersfield Portfolio, Queen's Quarterly, Qwerty* and *This Magazine.* Thanks to the editors of these publications / listening posts.

The publishers and the author
gratefully acknowledge the support
of the Canada Council for the Arts.

The publishers are grateful for the
support of the Ontario Arts Council.

Wolsak and Wynn Publishers Ltd.
192 Spadina Avenue, Suite 315
Toronto, ON
Canada M5T 2C2

National Library of Canada Cataloguing in Publication Data

McOrmond, Steven Craig, 1971-
        Lean days / Steve McOrmond

Poems.
ISBN 0-919897-94-0

        I. Title.

PS8575.O741.42 2004   C811'.54   C2004-900220-1

for

John Smith

Contents

Loyalist Burial Ground

So Long

The Blue Hills

The Discography of Silence (Poems about Glenn Gould)

Loyalist Burial Ground

Loyalist Burial Ground

You are fifteen. Nothing comes easy.
She is fragile as a night moth and touching her, you believe
some of that luminous sheen will come off on your hands.
Tomorrow you must pin a rose on her pale blue dress
without pricking the skin or appearing to notice
the shadowy place between her breasts like a pause in speech.
Across town, your grandfather is dying in hospital.
It is slow and painful, a little worse each day,
and you wish it would just be over.
When the tailor measured you – inseam, rise,
shoulders and sleeves – for your new black suit,
you hoped your penis wouldn't poke its head out and squeal.
Sleep brings bad dreams when it comes at all,
so you sneak out of the house and shelter here
among the headstones – loops and cursive of lichen,
a calligraphy of absence. You try on adulthood
to see how it fits, practise saying *I love you* and *goodbye*.

The dead

don't want to let go
any more than you do:

smell of their hair and skin
in dresser drawers and closets,

that voice in the street
turning your head.

And though they have become
something less than the wind

doesn't mean they are harmless.
As shadows, as fingertips

touching your face, they wish you
no hurt but it is so much to bear –

not to join them there in the quiet
out of the rain and weather.

They know they should keep away
but can't help hounding:

whispers in an empty room, least caress
of the breeze. Asking you to choose.

Gruff and brown, my father

Gruff and brown, my father speaks
to skunks under the evening star —
a mother and her kittens flourish
tails between the cabbage rows.

My father leans on the spade, pitches
bread crumbs from his sweater pocket —
the little ones come, tumbling each over each.
Mama rustles the cabbage leaves.

The old man breathes heavily
the sweetness of hay bales and lilac.
Skunks sniff at the stars, meander on.
My father wipes his brow, mutters

good-byes before limping to the house.
My mother has paused a moment
at the kitchen window, her arms folded —
remembering his softness in the dark.

As if

They mattered, those years:
a one-streetlight town, fields
far as you could see –

        Saturday night,
half-tons cruise
Granville Street, farm-hands
lighting up the tires, steering
with their big fat penises.
Alice gives them the finger
and you both think you'll die

laughing. The Co-op closes at five
but you can buy cigarettes at the all-night
Texaco on the highway. Nothing much to do
but smoke your faces off, drink cheap wine
from the bottle and talk about boys.

Sex in his dad's Chev,
sticky vinyl and a ten-minute
Zeppelin song, hands sure and methodical
like he's adjusting your carburettor – he's studied
parts and service in *Hustler*.
The best you can hope for is
to fall in love, marry
a hockey player.

The sharpest memories hurt:
                 red glow
of a cigarette at 2 a.m. and how
the wheatfields at night were a wide

whispering sea. Years after,
opening your eyes in the middle of a bad
dream: the bottomless wheat
and Alice
slipping under.

Hometown: a letter

Steve, ever wonder what it's like to be the one
who stayed? I enter the past easily as slipping
naked into water the same temperature as air –
Scholten's convenience store on the corner, bootleg
fags and single condoms sold under the counter,
the barber shop on Regent St. where we got trims
before our Coronation dance, now an adults only
video store, windows papered over with pink tissue.
I saw in the *Gleaner* that someone's been stealing
shrubs from Forest Hill Cemetery, digging up
their ganglia of roots and sod, leaving potholes.
Remember that hot August afternoon we
cycled there to visit Alden Nowlan sleeping under
his simple Celtic cross, took turns reading his poems
aloud and in lieu of flowers, sprinkled wine – *here,
Alden, you must be thirsty*. Today it's cold and rainy,
the river flooding its banks and the army bussed in
from Gagetown to lay sandbags. God, what I wouldn't give
for you to be sitting in Young's with me now, three eggs,
bacon, sausages, hash browns, a side of home-made
baked beans. The Hungry-man breakfast a far cry
from Toronto's *petit déjeuner*. At College and Bathurst,
I bet it's already 20 degrees. I picture you on a patio
getting drunk on sangria. In this town, spring is the cruellest
season, sinking its teeth in your bones. I'll console myself
with Saturday's paper, the crossword. A bottomless cup.

Loyalist Burial Ground II

Misery wants someplace to hide. Friends and strangers
crowded into your kitchen, their talk and laughter
a limb of light stretching across the lawn, you duck out,
cut through the neighbour's flower bed and onto George Street.
Rows of dark houses. Somewhere a cat yowling in heat.
Hop the wrought-iron fence, mindful of spikes – dull, ornamental
but they can pin you to the sky. Find an unlit corner
among crumbling stone crypts, a tree to lean against.
About those early settlers, you could care less.
You come here to clear your head and to smoke.
They stopped at this bend in the river
to await a winter like nothing they had known.
Most pitched tents and died. You light a cigarette,
look up through branches and twitchy leaves.
Here the dead stay dead. It's the living
who haunt us – you had your first serious
conversation here at two in the morning,
came back later to make love, your bodies
delicate as blown glass. A week ago she told you
she loves another. You want to lash out,
kick and topple the tombstones, but a heaviness
holds you to the ground. Too tired even to shed a tear.

Apprehension

Walking in the quiet not long after dawn, you find
deer tracks in the soft clay of the old railway bed,
squat down and trace the hoof prints
as though some of the deer's presence
might rub off and leave you
subtly changed. Evidence of another life
going on outside your own. This is the season
of men dressed in bright orange vests, white-tailed bucks
tied to the roofs of cars. And yet the deer
travel the abandoned tracks into the centre of town,
bending under the ghostlight of stars
to nibble windfall apples on the courthouse lawn.
They inhabit whatever margins we leave for them
completely. You want to follow
the deer's spoor as far as it takes you, a buck or doe
feeding quietly on browse. But your gaze could scarcely be
much different than that of the bank manager,
the owner of the hardware store, squinting
through the scope of a high-powered rifle,
lining up the cross-hairs. Predator, lover, devourer,
maybe it isn't too late for you to learn
to keep your distance and love
something you must not touch.

Loyalist Burial Ground III

During the day, squirrels chatter and scurry
among the headstones, telling you to quit
reading *memento mori* in everything.
But at this hour, the squirrels are gone
wherever squirrels go. You linger
over faint inscriptions carved in stone
nearly two centuries ago, the texture of erasure.
The dead have no names. Mute longing
seeps like dampness from the earth.
Sometimes all we're meant to know
is the ache of loss. Smell of her hair,
birthmark on her knee curved like a comma.
Welcome to Dumpsville, population: you.
Limbs heavy, tongue thick, you can imagine
living with this illness a long time. At first
you could find no end to it, memory a fishhook.
But lately there's a dull shine, light hardening
in the distance. A day when you show your scars
proudly. She loves you, she loves you no longer.

Patricia, as I stand

Patricia, as I stand in line behind the hearse,
is nine years old and hops from the car
in a rush of blue satin. She is suddenly
pressed into me – I collapse
in the squeeze of her arms
and huge eyes – sad gift among monuments.

Patricia, her sister in the coffin and no tears,
holds me, face in my belly, and whispers:
You told us stories, Amanda liked your stories.
I hold her tighter – moments
before she leaves me and
Amanda goes to the ground.

Loyalist Burial Ground IV

Ever since you quit smoking, you don't know what to do
with your hands. When a group of teenage girls lights up,
the voice in your head says screw the Surgeon-General.
What harm could it do you now with your body's
routine infidelities? Spare tire, trick knee.
The girls are joined by a boy in baggy jeans, hooded
sweatshirt. They stand around talking, one girl
leans against a monument, another trails her hand absently
along the smooth stone. The boy starts to goof around,
feeling pent-up in his skin. Maybe
you should stop staring — *ok, mister,*
let's get those hands up where we can see 'em.
But you couldn't drag your eyes away if you tried.
The tall skinny boy with the shaved head
is so in love with the dark-haired girl he can't
hide it, her distant smile keeps him up at night.
Your one wish is that they love each other simply
and fiercely for as long as it lasts. It's getting late,
dusk settling in the trees, shadows slanting from headstones.
The girl with the dark hair has someplace to go.
She starts walking, and what choice does he have
but to follow, the star of her cigarette pointing the way.

The coming of lean days

Walking in woods near Gagetown, we uncover a conspiracy among the birches and poplars, each leaf a whispering tongue. Spruces harden their hearts, fill up with resin. Early in October, fallen leaves, twigs and debris, fungal networks, worms. Add rain and the litter layer steeps: mushrooms, their gilled undersides, puffballs, cup fungi, stinkhorns. Although it's still warm enough to take a dip in the river, we are filled with premature nostalgia. When winter owns the real estate, all will be famine.

Back home, sunset after a day of showers turns the walls fiery orange. The half-empty wine bottle awash in light. Its afterimage on the wall, part shadow, part molten glow. We watch a spider spinning a web in the window. Seven stories above the ground, it pays out its precarious geometry.

Next morning, crows pierce the gauze of sleep. Hunched in treetops, they are grumpy old men. Their raucous gossip and sexual innuendo. We crawl out of bed and start the coffee. The spider's web is finished, glazed with night's perspiration. Already a few flies caught in the gooey strands.

Baubles of wind, we are all hanging by a thread.

The burn barrel

Late October morning,
fields furred with frost,
a film of ice on puddles.
Your job to awaken the beast
from its dreamless sleep, light a match
and watch as it sputters,
                              spits
              sparks.

The plastic bags melt away,
their contents spill hissing
into the barrel – butcher paper
soaked through with blood, milk
cartons, snotty Kleenex, turkey leg
used to make soup, flames licking
what little flesh is left on the bone.

                    You must stay
until everything is smoke and char.
Envelopes with their official correspondence
enclosed, your brother's dirty magazines,
the centrefold shrivelling before your eyes.

You've learned that all things
can be made to disappear. Last season's
Sears catalogue, thicker than the family Bible
and more thumbed over, a book of ash
that shatters when a puff of wind
tries to turn the pages.

Broken country

Winter has been gnawing on an old bone
and this is the bright idea it's come up with:
                    two foxes,
kinetic on the snow-field,
arrest you from the white
monotony and mindless
rhythm of your skis.
                    They burn
against the backdrop,
noses hoovering back and forth
just above the snow.

If you could get near,
you'd see their eyes glow
luminous dull green
even though no strong light is shining into them.

How to describe things
when language is little else but hunger:
metaphor, lurching, attempts to close
the distance between words and what is always other.
                    It crashes
up to its belly in snow.
You shift cold bones in your skin.
                    Suddenly,
wind swirls and the foxes smell you in it.
Disappointment and desire.
                    They streak
across the field toward a stand of evergreen,
spruce and Jack pine,
their tails trailing like clouds.

Crocuses

Because the corms stiffen
until stocky like weight-lifters
they heave themselves up –
fissure the earth, dislodge
clumps of frost hard clay.

Because the meek accept
the lion's share of the burden,
they are surly and headstrong:
spiny leaves and crustaceous
claw-like stems,
all thick skin and fleshy purpose.

Soon the taut buds
will muscle into bloom, stigmas
stained the deep orange-yellow of saffron,
exuberant foot soldiers of a new regime.
Because they are among the first
to break the ground.

Loyalist Burial Ground V

It's a warm day in May. The girl cuts class
to bum smokes and change for a bus ticket to Moncton.
Pink hair and pierced navel, she sits cross-legged
atop the crypt of some soldier or shop-keep,
smoking a cigarette and waiting impatiently for her lover
whose eyes are as blue and vacant as the sky. She is eager
to pull him close, run fingers up and down
his forearms. Together they will feel their way through the dark
passages and chambers of the heart. It hurts a little
to look at her. Were you ever so headstrong or full of light?
A few weeks ago, the first crocuses burst through
the thin rime of snow, grasping like claws. As suddenly,
home has become a place to leave. Her parents are kind but
                                                                          unbearable.
There is nothing this town can teach her that she doesn't know
already. Desire is a toothache. When she closes her eyes,
she sees skylines: Halifax, Montreal, Vancouver. It doesn't matter.
The girl checks her watch, takes a last drag of her cigarette
and tosses the butt. Seen from a distance, she might be blowing a kiss.

So Long

Departure sensitive

for Janet

These days, each window casts a rhombus of sunlight on the floor, brightens, dims, then brightens again, glowing like tungsten.

Love's horrible. All you can think about is fucking that person. Or you catastrophise. The future's an unreleased Russian film, storms of Stalin and wheatfields, wheatfields flattened under boots. Worst case scenarios when you're conspicuous by your absence.

You asked last night, 'Are you fearless?' I was trying to seduce you to stay and I laughed, 'I am full of fear.'

Do you know your hands flit and rest a moment on my shoulders and I can't think of pain and a time after pain? Only now and now – no, I'm lying. I'm a chipmunk filling his cheeks for the long winter ahead. I store you up in my memory, in my mouth and skin, in case things don't work and I'm cold, starving.

It took a tall drunk guy in a blue dress to tell me I have great lips. It took you to show me who they were made for. You came and you said, 'I am for you, for now.' You came and said, 'I will be everything you asked for, and else, and more.'

Today, lying on my back, I've decided I will be fearless. So the future's a Russian flick. I will not go to see it. The window's open. This wind that licks my skin and runs its fingers through my hair is warm without a hint of winter. And if I get up and go to the window...Yes.

Watching a woman drying herself

I would fly from December's cold bones.
South America dangles like a piece of fruit.
Lima, Santiago, Buenos Aires, the cities
of desire. I would dance you down
the crooked spine of the Andes, climb

Brazil's high plateaus, cut a path in
to mists and animal cries. Understory
where margay slinks on soft paws,
and *el tigre* whom the Indians call
jaguara is ghost of the forest.

I would take you here to swelter
in a close room of rain, by the trickle
of Amazon, screeching
chorus of green and cobalt blue
macaws. Wet to the skin, love,

I would begin, meticulous
as a cartographer, memorising
folds and contours, flat plane of
your stomach and the valley
between peaks my tongue

is hungry to name. Macaws startle the air,
turn sky to mosaic, *jaguara* pursues
a scent through rain. You are lush fruit,
the perfume of fruit. Return with me
into warm mists, our teeth into ripeness.

Calm

You've taken off your shirt and bra to feel the sun's heat on your breasts. Eyes closed, head thrown back, basking. Sounds of mid-autumn drift in and out. Squirrels busy in the treetops, someone hammering shutters into place.

This is your favourite time. When most of the summer people have gone home to their busy lives. By now, the bored teenager who blasted her boom-box all of July must be enrolled in drivers-ed. How thrilled she must be to step behind the wheel of her own affairs. So long.

Sudden whine of an outboard motor. Two fishermen must have drifted down the lake, caught sight of you on the shore, and decided to get a good look. They've cut the throttle and bob about twenty yards off the dock.

One man looks to be in his seventies, wisps of white hair. The other is perhaps fifty and just starting to turn grey. Two grown men (father and son?) crouched in the boat, grinning at one another like schoolboys.

Maybe the son has taken the day off to help close the cottage. Bleed the plumbing, haul the boat out of water. The old man is getting shaky and the son knows it. So what can he do when his father suggests they take 'er out for one last trip?

Now the sight of a woman with her top off drags them from the thoughts they share and for which neither can find the words. You suppose you should feel indignant, cover yourself, give them the finger. But already you sense they feel foolish and a little afraid.

The younger man fumbles in the tackle box for his smokes and a light while the old man sees to the outboard. It's been acting up lately, needs coaxing. But this time – *thank Christ* – the old engine coughs and sputters, starts to purr and they churn from sight. Long after they've gone, you're still looking. Sun-dappled water. Calm. Perhaps the last warm day of the year.

Postscript

That sound you took for someone pounding shutters in place might also have been a dull axe thudding into hardwood, the grain stubborn. But it wasn't this either. From someplace deep within the tumult of autumn leaves comes the rhapsodic, subtropical cry. You're positive it's a Pileated woodpecker, crow-sized and implausible, hammering into an oak tree. Your desire to see one – head bobbing mechanically like a cartoon character as the short, sturdy beak tastes wood again and again – is what drags you out of the Muskoka chair, shirtless, breasts swaying, to scan the tree tops. Planets of green, red and yellow that shift and ruffle like the surface of water. *Keek keek keek keek keek*. A conjurer drawing a rope of painted scarves from his throat. The birth of magic realism in a cold country. It isn't long before the men show up in the motorboat and ruin everything. You never did glimpse that woodpecker that left its name quivering up there in the high branches. And you won't see another for years.

Turbulence

You hate flying —
toys made of balsa
poised on god's fingertip.

Shortly after takeoff
our finger of air
drops out from under,
an oxygen mask falls
into a fat woman's lap —
oh sweet jesus.

The next instant
finds us back on course
but holding hands so
tight the nails
dig in. Suddenly

no time left for
argument or apology.

Stand by
   for J.

Waited while they de-iced the plane. Waited while the flight crew struggled down the gangway and into the terminal, bent almost double against wind and freezing rain. Now the jet sits on the tarmac – everything shot through with a wild diffuse light – and it looks like I won't be home tonight.

To pass the time, I thumb through your copy of *Running in the Family*. Look up now and then to watch the weather's progress. Ploughs and trucks clearing and salting the runways, clearing and salting, for what? The storm's stalled. It's not going anywhere and neither are we.

The words keep me warm. Wilpattu jungle, tea plantations on the verge of monsoon, gardens of cactus and flowering succulents. Turn the page and walk through the gate into a lush green zone. Hidden in the midst of this jittery waiting and snow, a Jaffna afternoon. Blades of a ceiling fan. Dream-like slowness. Faint ripples in the heat.

Words – how Ondaatje has his muscular way with them – and how your thoughts move in the gaps until I can't see the work as anything but an intimate collaboration. Notes in the margins have faded since the CanLit course at Trent, but it's still possible to follow the blaze of your intelligence through the slim elegant text.

Weigh your scribbled phrases in my mind as if they were mangoes. Ripe oblongs of intuition. Passages beside which you can pencil only an exclamation point. Here the lines permit nothing but awe: *It is delicious heat. Sweat runs with its own tangible life down a body as if a giant egg has been broken onto our shoulders.*

Once on a walk downtown to meet Andy and Paul, Dave and Sue, you stopped to smell the honeysuckle, mock-orange and fragrance laden lilac. And finally a huge white blossom fringed with pink and purple, its stem buckling under the weight of extravagance. It gnawed at you because you couldn't remember what to call it.

Hours later in the middle of a dull conversation about academe, the name fluttered down on soft silent wings and perched on your shoulder. *Peony,* it sang and before anyone noticed was gone.

Field guide

for Don McKay

Because it is a marvel of complexity and miniaturisation.

Because it is precious and fragile and once damaged cannot be
　　　repaired.

Because there is a bridge of bones across which vibrations rattle like
　　　freight cars.

Because it is an ecology unto itself.

Because they have been spotted as far north as Labrador.

Because it is strange to think of its humble beginnings: bones of the
　　　reptilian jaw hinge.

Because they are connoisseurs of the squawk, the warble, the trill and
　　　the whoop – to say nothing of the lick, the chop, the wow and
　　　the wah-wah.

Because it is hopelessly in love with saxophone and the crack of a bat.

Because it finds your flutters and fibrillations resistible.

Because it is the shy sister of fairy-tales: like Cordelia, it 'loves and is
　　　silent.'

Because it is an organ with 30,000 keys.

Because it is housed in a concert hall the size of a pencil eraser.

Because they are small and secretive. Because they neither show nor
　　　tell.

Because it is shaped like an abalone shell.

Because it smells like the sea.

Because they are barometers made of flesh and bone.

Because it is smaller than the head of a match yet it experiences no
　　　performance anxiety.

Because they are endangered.

Because silence has been poured into them – as has lead.

Because even standing still requires miraculous feats of balance and
without its two tiny sacs, you wouldn't have a leg to stand on:
no doing the shimmy at the wedding dance, no choo-choo
and boogaloo.

Because its canal is 2.5 cm in length and reminds one of Venice.

Because it lends itself.

Because it can be so eclectic in its tastes: Mahler and Bill Evans,
plainsong of water travelling through pipes, wind in the
alders, acid jazz.

Because of the woman upstairs practising the cello.

Because it is what Georgia O'Keeffe had in mind when she painted
Two Calla Lilies on Pink.

Because it can be restless and needy as the tongue.

Because it hungers for lost songs: dodo, curlew, auk.

Because together they make the most improbable of wings.

Ellis Portal

for Matthew Tierney

Matt, your letter written on translucent paper is an origami bird with folded wings. Small miracle that it finds me here in the city where I am learning to make peace with my brave new life. A basement apartment with all the charm of a root cellar: potatoes sprouting in the cupboard, mould on the towels. A job that merely pays the bills. Of all the news I have to tell, none of it is mine: Karl is busking up and down the coast of California. Jane just moved to Madrid. Darcy is spending the summer on a sheep farm in Tasmania. About as far away as I can imagine. When I see a jet climbing out of Pearson, I believe I should wave: everyone I ever loved, or who ever loved me, settling in for the long flight. I've read that, in sleep, muscles relax and the eye assumes the shape suitable for distant viewing. Next month in Beijing, you'll board the Trans-Siberian Railway, travel north through Mongolia, across Siberia and into Moscow. A day and a half to traverse the Gobi Desert by train. I finish your letter and hold it up to see how the light shines through.

§

Some mornings the queue to buy lottery tickets
is as long as the line-up for the train.

It rolls into the station, blast of stale sub-
terranean wind and we board, shuffling our feet.

Hear the familiar three note chime, descending
triad in B-flat major. The doors are closing.

First notes in the hook from Jesus Christ Superstar,
opening of the Sesame Street theme: *Sun-ny day...*

§

When I first moved to the city after a succession of small towns, Dave took me to an Indian restaurant where we met his friends. The waiter struck a long wooden match and lit the floating candle in the centre of the table. I opened the menu and said to a woman, "You know, I've never had Indian food before, I don't know what to order." She ordered for me – Naan, Saag chicken, Aloo Gobi. Her dress was sheer as water. Next morning in Kensington Market, I handled the blood oranges and pomegranates with her in mind.

§

In Japan
the animals speak
another, older language: cats *neow*,
little dogs *cancan* and frogs *garugaru*.

Fucking strange, eh?

Matt

§

The mess we make of our lives
given half a chance:

a giant of a man screams into a pay phone
while two transit cops stand warily

waiting for this fire to burn itself out
or for something more serious to happen.

Downstairs a trio is playing Pachelbel,
the man's fury mingles with baroque:

the violin's mixture of signature harmonics
and necessary complications: zing

as bow hits string, the musicians' chairs creaking
as inexorable music lifts and shakes their bodies.

§

During the months of July and August, when facilities on the
mountain are open, thousands make the climb each day and each
night. Now it's late October, the off-season, and you're determined to
scale Mount Fuji before you leave Japan. You take a bus two hours
from Tokyo to Kawaguchiko, from there a taxi to the fifth level at
about 2,300 meters, where the climb begins. Three hours and you
don't see another soul. Three hours and you hear nothing but the wind
and your own breathing. Remarkable for Japan! How will you describe
this experience later when the right words exist only in Basho or
Buson?

Stars and moon.
        Give me something
                poetic. I can't quite get it...

                        Matt

An hour from the summit, you join a small band of exhausted foreigners. Too tired to speak, you are sleepwalkers travelling together through a dream. Arrive suddenly in the midst of a small village, boarded up and bleak. This is not what any of you expected. Pass through the wooden gate that leads onto the crater rim. A weather station. A shrine. Wind so strong you can barely stand. You watch the sunrise from Fujisan — something immense and not of our making heaves into focus — and you feel like weeping. A few hours rest and then back down to earth.

§

Local proverb: he who climbs Mount Fuji once is a wise man, he who climbs it twice is a fool.

§

Where I come from, it is impossible to remove yourself from the drama of weather and seasons. Summer has the sweet smell of cut hay. Purple loosestrife, ragweed, vetch. Often pesticides leave yellow gum on cars. If it isn't washed off, it will burn down to the bare metal. In the fall, there are lights in the fields long after dark, farmers and hands working to bring in the harvest. One day soon winter will arrive and against everyone's wishes decide to stay. When I was a boy, snowdrifts reached as high as the power lines. Storms left us without electricity for days. Puddles of light from the oil lamps, smell of wet wool in the kitchen and the wood stove's insatiable appetite. A Polaroid of my father bravely setting out for work in the yellow Volkswagen. Narrow chasm between steep walls of snow, the track barely wide enough for one car. After long captivity, we emerge into spring as though out of the ground. We are thin and pale as shoots.

§

The bus is half empty when the man
twitchy and ferret-like eases himself

into the seat beside the woman,
blonde hair and tortoise-shell glasses.

His tongue is unappeasable. It darts
again and again to moisten parched lips.

He inches closer. She yawns,
pulls a book from her bag and begins to read.

§

These things make the city bearable: used bookshops crammed floor to ceiling, the smell of paper and must. Stopping for a hotdog on the street. The view of the city from the ferry as it crosses to Hanlan's Point. The cubist skyline – our works and deeds – appears more impressive even as it recedes. The spicy exoticism of Indian, Ethiopian, Thai and Laotian food. How you can adjust your watch by the Korean shopkeep who each night precisely at ten locks up, drags garbage to the dumpster. The homeless man downtown who sells tiny soap carvings of angels. Hiking with a friend in the ravines, lush green conduits snaking beneath the city. Hiddenness and wonder. Making the pilgrimage to see two peregrine falcons that have taken up residence on the steeple of St. James Cathedral. That these rare wild creatures should trade open country for windshear canyons of glass and steel. *Peterson's Field Guide* says that the peregrine is a swift falcon of nearly world-wide distribution. The Latin *peregrinus*, foreigner, from abroad. From which we derive the adjective *peregrine,* travelling or migratory.

§

The woman agape and pointing. Look:
up through the smog-filled air, the falcons.

§

Stars and moon, Matt. Stars and moon.

§

An overcast Saturday filled with ozone and sharp light. All afternoon, I apply a thin film of myself to the triage of editing poems. Rock doves scurry up and down the steep metal roof of the building next door. Nails on chalkboard. Though they mate for life and trace their lineage back to the biblical symbol of peace, they're the birds everyone loves to hate. Bang on the window, they fly away, return to shit on the balcony. Incorrigible creatures of habit. Later, screech of brakes, excited voices on the street. One of the doves struck by a car hobbles in circles dragging a mangled wing. People are standing around wondering what to do. Someone has gone to call the Humane

Society. A girl is moved almost to tears as the bird tries again and again to fling itself back into the air. Its wing a tattered sail, bones broken flutes, yet the heart pumps and the body wills itself onward. In those terse moments before the light leaves, it wants what we all want. The world.

The Blue Hills

Almost

Since you've been gone, we've relaxed
the rules around here: Ginsberg's allowed
to sleep on the bed. I think we both
appreciate the company. Thump of his heart,
his heat and shaggy bulk
filling the gap – almost.

Only problem is he chases rabbits,
whimpers and twitches like he's
having nightmares: ole Ginz
making evasive manoeuvres, fleeing a bunny
big as the backyard, a chip
on its shoulder.

I should talk.
I toss and turn most nights,
tail between my legs, trying to dodge
the home movies looping
through my head. Nothing like
a little melodrama: words and wine glasses
thrown in my direction, some scenes they hit,
some they miss.

And as if this wasn't enough,
the terror I keep waking from: your voice
calls across the ocean between us.
I walk on water, I stumble
over the blue hills
endlessly toward you.

How-to

He tries but Christ,
the boy's scared shitless of the power saw
and you know yourself, he couldn't
swing a hammer to save his life. My father's voice
climbing the stairs to where I lay
tucked in bed — me and my smashed thumb.

Sure don't take after his old man, he'd sigh,
not without a little pride but lately,
seems like I only remember *Ben Weider's*
Weight Lifting, a kid's Christmas
present from his dad — *Let's see*
some muscles, eh? — that and a screwdriver set.

                    Pop,
if you could see me now: *all feet,*
teeth, and eyeballs, same as then. Your son
still can't hang a picture straight, much less
fix his busted marriage. I keep thinking
you'd know exactly what to do, how to
make the hinges flush. I only wish
I had your wherewithal.
And muscles.

Mid-January

Cold enough
to freeze the nuts off a steel bridge.
Bundle up, pretend
it's that summer, camping out
on the beach near Rustico.
You hadn't been to the Island
since you were a teenager and I
was happy to play tourist.
We did it all: saw Anne, ate compulsory
lobster in a church basement.
But most I think of lying
next to you in the sleeping bag: I try to
sense where you begin, where
my limbs merge with yours or trail
into flannel. Drowsily watching
the campfire, familiar ballads
fumble through the pines, drunken
musicians, stars and guitars
play into the hands of morning.
                                    Did it really
happen like this, or
am I doing it again? So what
if it sounds like a Harlequin — some wine with that
cheese? It's better than this
lump in the throat: could have done,
if only.

Full blast

Between sips of lemonade, your mum
tells how, four years old, you squared off
with the Ukrainian neighbours'
German shepherd, the poor beast
chained up and hungry: *watch
your fingers! Well, didn't she march over,
look him dead in the eye
and make friends?*

But then you've never been
faint of heart – except for flying and now
this fear of rats:
                          Awake
in the cellar of your worst
imagining, the house
collapsing on top of you, gas
stove, kitchen chairs and cupboards,
toilet with its plumbing
going nowhere: *help
I can't move.*

How many hours, days
before a faint stirring
opens your eyes? You squint
into absolute blackness, the sound
gets louder, white
noise like tape-hiss, like lying
in the cone of a bass speaker, last track
over and the silence turned

full blast. You've heard it before,
know what's coming, no
rescue team with pry-bars
and lights on helmets –

                something
unspeakable: furred dark,
massive, slavering, and oh so
eager to deliver you,

                piecemeal,
back to earth.

Predawn

Unburying the silver hush
between lovemaking and sleep, your touch
is an inquiry. Fingertips trace
designs on my face, make flesh
an artefact, old intrigue
consumes you – archaeologist

quietly manic in the arc
light of the moon, you labour to unearth
a lexicon, intimate yet unheard.
What remains, barest of impressions, will
carry the whole of an evening; you
pursue prehistory, the dark

ages before you.

Bacon and eggs

Back into the schmaltz again,
I try to quit but desire
pricks the skin, pushes the plunger.
Fog drifts in and when it clears
I'm somewhere else, with you: the great
apartment on St. George, our first —
crumbling ceilings, faint bouquet of
mildew and catpiss.

It's a lazy Sunday, Handel's
Messiah on the stereo, bacon and eggs
served on chipped plates, strong coffee
to waken our limbs — you stretch
across the table, rub sleep from my eye.
We begin to clean up,
                 you wash,
I dry.
Wait for you to finish the frying pan,
my nose buried in the nape of your neck — ah,
fernspice, musk rose. You lean
toward my kisses, deliver
the heavy iron skillet into my hands.
The warm bubble of air
around us trembles —
       hallelujah.
Bursts.

Last night

I walked out
with Ginsberg chasing
terns along the harbour
and you called

these days the machine
talks to you
more than I do

spent nearly an hour
trying to get through before
I fell asleep on the sofa

last night, greedy
I dipped into you
over and over
like gulls

The Discography of Silence
(Poems about Glenn Gould)

A bird doesn't sing because it has an answer – it sings because it has a song.

Chinese Proverb

Please don't tell me it all adds up in the end.
I'm sick of that one.

John Ashbery,
"Variations on 'La Folia'"

Glenn Gould recording the Goldberg Variations in New York, 1955

To coax the bird to fly
in the narrow corridors of its cage
and woo some meaning, however fugitive,
from this nothingness of tones. To bring us closer,
exquisite creatures of logic
and emotion. To reach the end
of all human possibilities, ashes and dust,
and begin again. Repetition
with variation. To find the key
that opens the sky
and demand of the gods
an audience.

Little G.G. in a northern prospect

The dogs have wandered off,
scent to scent, the air
filled with messages. He is a boy again
alone on the edge of frozen Lake Simcoe.
Strangely unencumbered by his father's heavy wool
coat and galoshes, he tests the ice,
a few steps. If he had the courage to walk across,
what would he find there on the far shore?
Cold, uncompromising brilliance. A city in ruins,
its inhabitants long since departed. The empty room
he entered when he first heard Beethoven.
A door swinging shut, the sound of cracking ice.

Slowness

At twenty-three, he knew nothing
except how to play the piano, his hands racing
toward the finish line. What he wanted was
to understand the inner workings
of a piece of music, to run his fingers
along its backbone, the shapely
underpinnings of ecstasy. To forget
about the instrument, audience, his own
slippery self, slow things down, lean into that
stillness and with the sad weight of his body
listen. What he wanted would take years.

His humming

In '55, it was barely
audible. The piano
merely a means to an end.

Only later, the instrument
could be a stranger
or an enemy.
The crowd out for blood.
It was vaudeville.
A monkey at the clavier.

Then his voice
could be heard at the back of the hall,
compensating for the failings
of strings and hammers.

The audience so near
he could smell them.
And Bach?
Conspicuously absent.

His debut at the Phillips Gallery, Washington, D.C., January 2, 1955

Two years
cloistered in the cottage
at Uptergrove. Only the dogs,
his piano and a tape recorder.
After the lessons and his falling-out
with Guerrero. The real work
as yet undone. You can take a bird into the house,
mend its wing, feed and sing to it,
and it may never fly. Two years
of warm-up, sore fingers
as he tested himself
again and again. The results
satisfactory, he sits
low in the improvised
bridge chair, coughs.
Begins.

Glenn Gould playing Brahms Concerto No. 1 in D Minor at extraordinarily slow tempi, 1962

Adagissimo. The tempo of stars.
Hovering over the Steinway, ghostly
white hands frozen above the keyboard – *wait,*
wait. Only silence
holds anything together. The razor's edge,
a kind of rapture.
These fingers that strike the keys
can't wait to leave them.

All-night recording session, 30th Street Studio, New York

Tense and anxious between takes, he soaks
his forearms in warm water, bullies the technician
to adjust the piano's action one more time
though he knows the problem has nothing to do
with bearings, levers, linkages.

Now, without warning, his fingers
in motion, each with a separate intelligence.
Attack and release – the endings of tones
as important as their beginnings.
                                    The notes
tingle at the base of the neck, quiver
across the scalp, over shoulders and down
the arms. His whole body humming, a receiver,
he smacks his lips together to keep pace, his cells
ready to explode if he doesn't
open his mouth and sing.

It's what he was made for, this
brief instant, the hammer in free flight
toward the strings, the final note as yet
unsounded. This capsule
of silence, a bird in space.

Glenn sprawled in the chair,
damp and panting, his brain ticking
like a car radiator as it cools.

The superintendent

Meeting for the first time in the elevator,
Gould covers his mouth with a handkerchief,
refuses to shake hands. She's been briefed
about the tenant on the top floor, otherwise
she might be inclined to stick him in the ribs
with the mop handle. Later he calls to explain
that someone is buzzing up, would she mind
going downstairs and telling whoever it is
to go away? When somebody tries to pry
open his mailbox and steal his letters,
she realises he must really be important.
From the beginning, theirs is a cold war, curt
pleasantries and palaver about the weather.
One night after her cleaning is done,
she decides to get some air, climbs the stairs
to the roof and is standing near his open window
when the playing begins. She leans against the ledge,
prepared to be bored stiff. The music makes her feel cradled
like a small child again, her mother singing her off
to sleep. She can think of nothing else she needs.
Almost every night now, she steals onto the rooftop.
He can play for hours without stopping.

Gould with Stravinsky and Bernstein

Three caged lions,
Glenn's there on the right,
the one not smiling.

No bones to pick with Bernstein.
Leonard's wife Felicia insisting
she shampoo and cut Gould's matted hair
before they sat down to dinner.

It was Stravinsky who rankled him.
The empiricist, his music inspired
only by the instrument. A mind so rooted
in the workaday, it forgets to dream.

If he ever had to choose
between a musical idea and a bowl of borscht,
Stravinsky would reach for a spoon.

'Hi, this is Glenn and I feel like talking'

He gets home late, slips off his shoes
and wades into the clutter, empty
milk cartons, orange juice containers,
mounds of unopened mail. Wandering
room to room in his stocking feet,
Pet Clark on the turntable
keeping him company.

                     Of all the things
to be afraid of – sleeping, not sleeping,
never waking up. Radio left on,
he dreams the hourly news bulletins,
music carrying from a long way off.

                     His mind veering
from its migratory corridors, stranding him
in a harsh landscape of taiga and tundra.
Sometimes he's seated at the Chickering
afloat on an ice pan headed for Labrador,
his old teacher Guerrero standing behind him
as he plays, hands on his shoulders
pressing down.
                Ah, Guerrero,
tonight your pupil is sorry
for the way he left things – that terrible reticence
between two people who have exhausted
all their words.

Hours before his body insists
it must lie down, he reaches for the telephone,
lifts it to his ear, then sets it back
in the cradle. It's after midnight, too late
to call. Hand still touching the receiver,
the only thing holding him to the world —
he dials a number,
                            waits.

CD 318

After the concert in Cleveland,
freight workers dropped CD 318
and she came apart at the seams.

He used to say the instrument
was of no great consequence. Sent back
to the workrooms, she would never be the same.

Now he thinks of Beethoven
sitting amid the wreckage of an early piano
that couldn't withstand his hammering.

When he first found her
in the basement of the Steinway building
on West 57th, he got down on his knees.

He only had to play for a moment
to know they were made for each other.

Platform antics

They expected him to sit up straight
like an operator at a switchboard

but it wasn't in the job description
to deny what the music wanted —

either to lift him up to heaven
or throw him broken to the floor.

They mistook him for a clown
in his rumpled suit and gloves with no fingers.

Later, for a vulture hunched over
the keyboard, disfigured by the thing he loved.

Nothing was for show: the gloves he wore
year round kept his hands at a constant temperature.

The folding chair, though it squeaked,
allowed him to sit low and strike the keys

flat-fingered. And when he hummed,
it was wishful thinking.

Fishing dispute

Holy Jesus, Herb, he's coming right for us!
The motorboat bearing down
                                                    full throttle.
At the wheel, this crazy
son of a bitch in a wool overcoat, yelling
at the top of his lungs, cap thrown back,
mouth stretched into an apocalyptic grin.
The scourge of Lake Simcoe.

Seconds before the shriek of
hull against hull, Gould cuts the wheel,
                                        the boat veers,
leaving the two fisherman
floundering in his biblical wake.
Herb nearly gets tossed in the drink.

If anyone asked him why,
he'd obfuscate: Even Bach, that powdered wig,
once walked more than 400 kilometres
to hear Dietrich Buxtehude play the organ.

For him, it was piano keys,
black and white: fishing was cruel
                                    and cruelty
must be fought in earnest.
Imagine the barb in your lip
tugging you out of your green depths until,
breaking the water's skin, alien space
rips down your length and the fillet knife
                                            dips.

Scherzo

Glenn Gould is a country so large it takes a week to cross by train.
Glenn Gould is 10,000 facts and contradictions flying in loose
      formation. The eccentricity of clouds.
Glenn Gould is a $400 dollar phone bill.
Glenn Gould is hockey night in Iqaluit.
Glenn Gould is a slow-moving disturbance. A cold coming on.
Glenn Gould is a fur hat stuffed full of learning or a fugue in
      F-sharp minor. Or maybe he is both.
Glenn Gould is a contrapuntal radio tuning in many stations at once
      without any perceptible static, the voices sailing over and
      under one another in an aerobatics display.
Glenn Gould is an idiot-savant who has stubbed his toe on the
      world.
Glenn Gould is the condition of remove – for which there is no cure
      in the pharmacopoeia.
Glenn Gould is the whine of high tension wires on a windy night,
      the crystal vibrato of stars.
Glenn Gould is a glass harmonica.
Glenn Gould is the discography of silence, mute longing of snow.
Glenn Gould is an ice floe the size of Texas that has broken away
      from the pack.
Glenn Gould is the fossil forest of Axel Heiberg. The memory of
      green persisting in permafrost.
Glenn Gould is a pair of wool socks with holes in the heels.

Glenn Gould is hunched over a table in the back of Fran's
 restaurant eating a cheese omelette and hash browns at three
 in the morning.
Glenn Gould is the quiet within order, a joy so cold it can stop
 the heart.
Glenn Gould is Aurora Borealis on a winter's night. (What does
 anyone really know about the Aurora Borealis?)
Glenn Gould is a soundproof room.

His favourite thing

He edges out into traffic
and presses hard on the pedal,
the polished hood of the Impala
long and wide as a concert grand.

Windows down, radio turned way up
above the growl of the big V8 –
carburettor sucking air,
turning it into horses, thrust.

This town he knows as intimately
as his own cock or Schönberg's piano pieces.
A city of hidden hills and six rivers
flowing to the lake. A city of churches.

One day, he'll just keep going:
Yonge Street slicing north and west
for 1,200 miles and Glenn never happier
than behind the wheel. A moving target.

North

Where a winter's night can be measured in years,
the distance between stars. Where breath
turns solid and the mind's never been
more fragile, drifting with the pack ice in a skin boat.
Where bright colours and the shiny
useless things that distract us
are sheared away, flesh from bone,
thought chipped to a spear point.
The economy of gesture, his voice
whispering: follow me.

Lake Simcoe, autumn, 1981

All week, caught in a state
of suspended agitation, updraft
and downdraft, they flashed like schools of fishes,
scales of yellow light. Until this morning,
packing up to go, it strikes him:
birches and poplars stripped bare,
                          the world
changed to something he can scarcely recognise.
The day sharp and toothy: cold drizzle, soot
from a stove burning green wood, chance
of flurries. Seen the wind? Who hasn't.

What he'll miss

Eggs and bacon at a roadside diner
a fast car parked outside, keys in the ignition.

The family cottage on the shore of a small lake
congenial silence and the crickets'

accidental music. How the wind plays
the bare trees of late autumn

as plaintive instruments. Fallen leaves
underfoot, the cidery smell of erasure.

The barn owl in flight, its wings' hush
a body sliding naked between sheets.

New snow. Hum and quaver of sodium
lights at dusk. The company of dogs.

Glenn Gould recording the Goldberg Variations in New York, 1981

After twenty-five years,
what did they expect to hear?
They will have to settle, as he has, for the windswept
coastline of Newfoundland, outports
approachable only by the sea.

Farther north: glacial slowness,
the possibility of perfection.
Months of darkness, then
the extravagant light of a summer day.
A herd of caribou
fording a river swollen with melt water.
                    Purple fugues,
the tiny flowers of Arctic Rhododendron
last no more than two weeks a year.

The blind alleys and hairpin turns
of the mind – how little these structures have changed
since the Stone Age. Creatures of distance
and desire, no longer
animals and not quite
gods.
                    Listen.
He is threading his way through the score
with an awl carved from polar bear bone.

Coda: Glenn Gould watches *Thirty-two Short Films About Glenn Gould*

Everyone should have the privilege
of seeing themselves on the big screen,
not just the precious and semi-precious,
but ordinary people like the tall thin boy
pouring sodas, buttering tubs of popcorn
in the concession stand. Certainly the small
details of this young man's life would be more
entertaining than his own. He has always been
disappointed by portrayals of the famous. This film
is no exception, although it's a strange feeling to observe
an actor inhabiting his skin, the resemblance
uncanny. Like looking in a mirror only the figure
staring back at you moves when you haven't
budged an inch. And oh what an actor –
so preternaturally handsome he would sit through
an entire film where nothing more happens than this
man sleeping, rising to shave, boiling water for tea.
Think what he could do playing the soda boy.
Anyone should have the right to pay
admission and watch their lives flickering
forty feet in the air while they eat their popcorn.
And it should happen while you are still alive
so you can go home afterwards, mull it over
and if you don't like what you see, change.

Notes on the poems

The poems about Glenn Gould owe a debt to the following works:

> Ackerman, Diane. *A Natural History of the Senses*. New York: Random House, 1990.

> McGreevy, John, ed. *Glenn Gould: Variations*. Toronto: MacMillan of Canada, 1983.

> Payzant, Geoffrey. *Glenn Gould: Music and Mind*. Toronto: Key Porter, 1984.

> Roberts, John P.L. and Ghyslaine Guertin, eds. *Glenn Gould: Selected Letters*. Toronto: Oxford UP, 1992.

The lines by John Ashbery used to introduce the Glenn Gould poems are taken from *Your Name Here*. New York: Farrar, Straus and Giroux, 2000. 49.

The italicised line in "Stand-by" is borrowed from Michael Ondaatje's *Running in the Family*. Toronto: General, 1984. 79.

"Ellis Portal" is named after Ellis Street, a small byway removed during the construction of the Yonge subway line in Toronto in the early 1950s.

"Patricia, as I stand" is for Patricia French, and in memory of Amanda French.

Acknowledgements

"As if" received second prize in *This Magazine*'s Great Canadian Literary Hunt (2001).

My thanks to Jan Zwicky and Don McKay for "the small / matter-of-fact miracle of ears."

Special thanks to Adrienne Barrett, Julie Dennison, Richard Lemm, David Seymour, John Smith, Matthew and Charmaine Tierney, and Andy Weaver for their invaluable editorial suggestions, friendship and support over the years.

Thanks to: Sabine Campbell, Paul Dechene, Ian Dennison, Bill Gaston, Renee and Ian Gattrel, Eric Hill, Bob and Margaret Hoops, Imperial Pub Library & Luba, The Ice House Writing Collective, Bill Kalogiros, Julie Kerr, Ross Leckie, Frank Ledwell, Molly's Coffee House, PEI Council of the Arts, Sue Sinclair, Tracy Staniland, Murray Sutcliffe, UNB Arts Centre, The Writer's Federation of New Brunswick, and to my parents, Edward and Mina McOrmond, with love and admiration.

Janet: "It is as though I wrote in a foreign language that I am suddenly able to read. Wordlessly she explains me to myself; like genius she is ignorant of what she does" (Jeanette Winterson). Thank you.